8-6

Guillaume Apollinaire

by LEROY C. BREUNIG

Columbia University Press
NEW YORK *&* LONDON 1969

LᴇROY C. BREUNIG is Professor of French at Barnard College.

Copyright © 1969 Columbia University Press
SBN: 231–02995–0
Library of Congress Catalog Card Number: 79–92030
Printed in the United States of America

Guillaume Apollinaire

"There are three Polish writers known today, and none of them writes in Polish: Conrad in England (he has talent), Przybyszewsky in Germany, and myself in France." Apollinaire thus described himself in a letter in 1915. His real name was Kostrowitzky, which his fellow soldiers at the front quickly transformed into "Cointreauwhiskey." If it be true, as seems most likely, that Apollinaire's father was an Italian army officer, this would make him only half-Polish. Some biographers claim, although with little proof, that through the Aiglon he was the great-grandson of Napoleon. Picasso among others hinted that his father was a high dignitary of the Church, possibly the Pope; and if Apollinaire never denied such rumors it was simply that he loved nothing more than to let legends proliferate about him.

The facts are that Guillaume Apollinaire was born in Rome in 1880, the illegitimate son of a Polish miss, Angelica de Kostrowitzky, whose father was a minor official in the Vatican, and that he was baptized Guillelmus Apollinaris de Kostrowitzky. From his birth to his death in Paris on the eve of the Armistice in 1918 when, again according to Picasso, the last words he heard from his bed were "Down with Guillaume!"— it was the crowd on the Boulevard Saint-Germain shouting against the Kaiser Wilhelm—Apollinaire's life has made a fascinating subject for biography. He resembles such French poets as Gérard de Nerval, Rimbaud, Verlaine, and Jarry in whose lives biographers find a mystery more enticing than the

[3]

poetry itself. His unconventional childhood on the French Riviera; the terror that he and his younger brother Albert felt for their baccarat-playing mother, whom Max Jacob has described as a demoniacal coquette with a barking, raucous voice, swinging a dog whip and wearing jewels that looked like snails returning from a pawnshop; the sojourn in the Walloon, at Stavelot, with the boys posing as Russian princes while Angelica lost all her money in the gambling houses of nearby Spa; the year as a tutor in the Rhineland singing German folksongs, visiting Munich, Prague, Vienna, and courting Annie, the puritanical governess from Clapham outside London; the all-important meeting in 1904 with Picasso whose poetic counterpart he became for a decade, leading the avant-garde experimentation in poetry and defending the cubist painters in the Parisian press; his imprisonment on charges (proved to be false) of complicity in the theft of statuettes from the Louvre which earned him the reputation of being connected as a "Russian anarchist" with the theft in 1911 of the *Mona Lisa*; the series of clandestine *erotica* he published in order to earn a few francs; his life as a soldier, feverishly writing epistolary poems from the front-line trenches until a German shell fragment pierced his skull and made him a Left Bank hero with bandaged head, the idol of the dadaists and future surrealists as he sat on the terrace of the Café de Flore; his stormy love affairs with a painter, Marie Laurencin, whom he graciously called a "cubist," with a *grande dame* (Louise de Coligny-Châtillon), with a schoolteacher (Madeleine Pagès), and with a "pretty redhead" (Jacqueline Kolb) whom he married just a few months before his death—all this makes tempting fare for a scintillating biography of a most engaging figure, "a fellow of infinite jest, of most excellent fancy," and one of the few writers—Jean-Jacques (Rousseau) was another—whom

[4]

readers affectionately address by his first name. Unfortunately the charm of Apollinaire does not entirely explain the originality of his poetry.

His being half a Pole is in itself less important than that he was a hybrid. In a land whose major writers rarely doubted their pure Frenchness even in their revolt against it, as with Stendhal and Rimbaud, the case of Apollinaire is something of an oddity. It was by chance that the French language became his instrument. Instead of dragging her two boys to Monte Carlo, Mme de Kostrowitzky might have taken them to San Remo, Wiesbaden, Marienbad, Corfu, or any other resort well stocked with casinos. The education Guillaume received in Monaco was very solid, and the chauvinistic critics who have attributed the linguistic liberties in *Alcools* and *Calligrammes* to Apollinaire's ignorance of French are most disingenuous. Unlike that other foreigner in Paris, Picasso, who after a decade was still massacring his adopted tongue, writing "tableux" for "tableaux," "vien" for "bien," and "esculptures" for "sculptures," Apollinaire had a thorough mastery of the language, its grammar, its orthography, and its punctuation. True, when *Alcools*, his masterpiece, appeared in 1913 the main reason for the scandal it caused was the total absence of punctuation marks. Actually, however, the commas, semicolons, and periods had all been there up to the moment he corrected the final proofs, and only then in one of those cavalier gestures so typical of his manner he peppered the margins with the delta sign for "delete" alongside every mark. That most of the French poets since have followed suit would seem to vindicate his judgment.

It was precisely because of his assurance in French that Apollinaire felt free to throw in occasional foreign words and expressions (Hebrew, Italian, German, English) without that hint of self-conscious effort which one senses in T. S. Eliot's and even Ezra Pound's borrowings. Apollinaire loved the French language. Few poets—one thinks of Villon and Verlaine —have composed such beautifully limpid lines in the rigorous octosyllabic mold; but his love did not amount to idolatry. He had little of that sense of the immutable correctness of the language which even the most revolutionary French poets share. To a journalist who once asked him if it didn't annoy him to see his name constantly misspelled as "Appolinaire" he replied, "Je m'en fous." This foreigner who could twist its language at will was just what France needed at the turn of the century to recover from the effete "talcum powder style" (Ezra Pound) of the minor symbolists.

The peculiar circumstances of Apollinaire's birth were to have a deeper effect, however, since they color the very substance and structure of his poetry. For "Kostro," as his friends called him, was not only a foreigner, he was a bastard. And if he knew the name of his father he never divulged it. The mystery of his parentage haunted him. Who was he? In "Cortège" (*Alcools*) he writes:

> Un jour
> Un jour je m'attendais moi-même
> Je me disais Guillaume il est temps que tu viennes
> Pour que je sache enfin celui-là que je suis. . . .

Apollinaire was above all a lyric poet, and the bulk of his verse is in the first person. The elusiveness of the self and the emotions it excites constitute a dominant theme. Indeed he was one of the first and the most lucid among the hordes of writers—and readers—engaged in the search for their indefinable identities in this twentieth century.

His rootlessness generated an exhilarating sense of freedom. He felt bound by no traditions, no taboos. Whether or not he

[6]

inspired the character of Lafcadio in Gide's *Les Caves du Vatican*, as has been claimed, Apollinaire was a fine example of Gidean "disponibilité," that total willingness to experience new sensations and beliefs. But noninvolvement can weigh heavily, and just as often we find him thirsting after more binding ties. What made the so-called *Mona Lisa* affair so traumatic was the fear of being deported from France, and the main reason perhaps for volunteering in 1914 was the prospect of automatically becoming a French citizen.

Such oscillation in turn reveals a deeper trait in Apollinaire, his congenital indecisiveness. Coming from no direction, he knew not what direction to go. A recurrent image in his poetry is the compass pointing in all four directions at once. In one of his little quatrains of *Le Bestiaire*, entitled "L'Ecrevisse," he apostrophizes "incertitude," calling it his delight and adding that "you and I" go along like the crayfish, "backwards." Aimlessness explains the workings of his mind as well, which was apparently unable to follow a neatly developed chain of reasoning. His thought proceeded by free association, hopping at random from one notion or image to another. The prose writing suffers from this fault. The two novels, *Le Poète assassiné* and *La Femme assise*, fail to achieve the coherence which this genre demands. The art criticism is inferior to Baudelaire's because it lacks the cogent expository style of the essays in *Curiosités esthétiques*.

Apollinaire might well have disintegrated into an inert mass of neutralizing contradictions but for his vigor and his lucidity. From someone (Napoleon?) he had inherited such intense energy that his indecisiveness, far from leading to Hamletism or apathy, produced a gargantuan desire to embrace all.

> Je suis ivre d'avoir bu tout l'univers
> ("Vendémiaire," *Alcools*)

[7]

(And he adds that he will drink it again if he likes.) Thanks to his lucidity he came to realize that in the very weakness of his undirected thought processes lay his strength and originality as a modern poet. He had only to transform "primitive disorder" (if we may adapt the terms of Kenneth Rexroth) into "sophisticated disorder."

It is obvious, of course, that during that fruitful prewar decade in Paris Apollinaire did make a choice—in favor of modernism. As spokesman for the new trends in painting and poetry in both the daily press and the little magazines he regularly defended whatever was the newest. This took a powerful lot of legerdemain, since Paris had never been so heady with "isms." They were sprouting on both banks: fauvism, neo-symbolism, unanimism, cubism, futurism, dramatism, orphism, simultanism, paroxysm, and the like. Apollinaire got involved in many internecine struggles and it took all his charm to placate his friends of one school who felt he had betrayed them for another.

Take for example cubism, undoubtedly the most important of these movements, which for certain literary historians encompasses a school of poetry as well as painting. Apollinaire was its most ardent champion in the press from 1910 to 1912, but between the completion of his manuscript for *Les Peintres cubistes* (1913) and the correction of the proofs he became fascinated by the canvases of one of the earliest abstract painters, Robert Delaunay. Sensing the importance of this new "pure painting," he decided then and there to call it "orphic cubism" and added the new category to the proofs. Then, only ten days after the book appeared, he announced that cubism had given way to "orphism" pure and simple. "The reign of Orpheus has begun." This of course incensed the cubists, and a year later when Apollinaire lauded the "futurism" of Delaunay he brought down upon him the wrath of Delaunay and futurists alike and came near provoking a duel.

What Apollinaire really espoused was avant-gardism. More important than the contents of this or that manifesto was the fact that what he championed was new. His most earnest desire was to form a common front in the fight against traditionalism, and his acrobatics with labels represent successive efforts by stretching the meaning of this or that "ism" to designate the over-all trends of the moment. The last label he sought to impose, without much success in spite of its greater accuracy, was simply "l'esprit nouveau."

Now the cult of newness can be not only superficial but downright dangerous as a way of life. For the poet, however, it can generate the enthusiasm, the sheer joy of singing what has never been sung before. In his 1917 lecture on the "new spirit" Apollinaire asked rhetorically:

> There's nothing new under the sun? I don't believe it.
> What! I had my head X-rayed. I've peered while alive into my own skull, and there's nothing new about that?
> Solomon was probably thinking of the Queen of Sheba, and he loved the new so much that his concubines were innumerable. . . .
> Perhaps for the sun there's nothing new . . . but for man . . . !

The Eiffel Tower, which the symbolists had ignored as a hideous new monstrosity, became for Apollinaire a gracious shepherdess guarding her bleating flocks, the bridges over the Seine ("Zone"). He presents the actual shape of the Tower typographically in some of his "calligrams," those picture poems which are the forerunners of today's "concrete poetry." In "Lettre-Océan" letters representing street sounds and objects are arranged in circles and radiating lines; it is only upon noting in the center the figure "300 metres high" that the reader suddenly realizes he is looking down upon the Tower as from an airplane. (Delaunay presents the same view in several of his paintings.) The airplane fills Apollinaire with the amazement of a child: it can actually land without folding its wings! All the latest discoveries of science find their way into his imagery. The real poets today, he claims, are the scientists; one of the first in France to pronounce the name of Sigmund Freud, he prophesied vast discoveries in the "abysses" of the human mind.

Unfortunately the new has the bad habit of never staying that way. The calligram of an automobile in "La Petite Auto" definitely betrays its 1914 lines, and Apollinaire's modernism, when only that, is paradoxically the element of his poetry that has aged most quickly, sounding at times like a not so felicitous mixture of Whitman and Marinetti. The spurts of old-fashioned optimism and the hopes in a bright future where the union of the spiritual and the technological will ensure the felicity of mankind seem woefully passé, and Apollinaire would be forgotten today were he merely the voice of the "Counter-Decadence" of the first decade and a half of the century.

His very rootlessness saved him, however, for among the contradictions it inspired was a fascination with the past just as intense as the anticipation of the future. A simple pirouette, and the Eiffel Tower becomes the Tower of Pisa. It is customary to divide Apollinaire's poetry into two neat categories, "Order" and "Adventure," using the terms he himself used in "La Jolie Rousse," his final "testament" in which he acts as moderator in the struggle between "tradition" and "invention." The poems of "Order," his biographers go on to say, are those carefully composed lyric pieces, usually in regular meter, love poems and *lieder* for the most part, in the tradition of Verlaine, Villon, or Ronsard. "Le Pont Mirabeau" is the classic example, and most of them date from the *Alcools* period. The poems of "Adventure" comprise all the experimental pieces, usually in free verse and stripped of a discursive framework. The most famous example is "Zone," the liminary poem of *Alcools*, although the last one to be composed (1912), which announces all the new ventures of the *Calligrammes* period.

This classification, while by no means false, especially as a very general chronological division, represents an oversimplification that can be misleading. Apollinaire began experimenting much earlier than 1912, and this includes the use of modernistic imagery—the Eiffel Tower pops up as early as 1902 —whereas *Vitam impendere amori*, a booklet containing some of the purest octosyllabic lines and traditionally tender, nostalgic sentiments, was published in 1917, the year of the lecture on the "new spirit." As a matter of fact, it is hardly accurate to speak of oscillation between "Order" and "Adventure," for the individual poems seldom fall exclusively into one category or the other but contain a mixture of both.

In any case mere dualities fail to explain the complexities of Apollinaire's inspiration. His spiritual ubiquity, his claim to be at once

> Au zénith au nadir aux 4 points cardinaux
> ("Merveille de la guerre," *Calligrammes*)

made him feel a deep affinity with the "fourth dimension" as he defines it in *Les Peintres cubistes*: "It figures the immensity of space eternalizing itself in all directions at a given moment." That this is hardly a scientific definition is beside the point; for Apollinaire it reflects in his poetry the constant effort to perfect a multidirectional style so as to express the intense radiation of his compass-boxing emotions. It is the stages of this effort that make up the chapters of Apollinaire's biography as a poet.

His first two known pieces, written at seventeen, are signed

[11]

"Guillaume Macabre," and indeed much of the early verse has the morbid tone of the *fin de siècle* which we associate with the symbolist movement. In symbolism Apollinaire also found nourishment for his love of out-of-the-way myths and fairy tales which he had had since childhood. Greek, Hebrew, and Celtic lodge side by side in these youthful efforts as they will in his first prose work, *L'Enchanteur pourrissant*. The death of Pan, the metamorphosis of Lilith into an osprey, the imprisonment of Merlin the magician under a crystal bell by the fairy Vivian, these are some of the rather decadent themes of this period.

Apollinaire excluded most of his teen-age works from *Alcools*, and we know them only through their posthumous publication in *Il y a*, *Le Guetteur mélancolique*, and "Poèmes retrouvés" in the Pléiade edition of the *Oeuvres poétiques*. Three fairly long poems which date from around 1900 have survived in *Alcools*: "Merlin et la vieille femme," "Le Larron," and "L'Ermite." The alexandrine quatrains and the narrative or (in the case of "Le Larron") dramatic form give them a deceptively neat, traditional appearance. Actually they are among the most enigmatic poems Apollinaire wrote. The obscurity comes in part from the strangeness of the three legendary characters (Merlin is the only one named): a hermit, a thief, and a magician, all of them representing of course the Poet. They are isolated figures who seem to exist out of time and place. The lack of localization recalls the symbolist manner which creates "landscapes of the soul" through the filtering process of the poet's memory.

Yet these pieces differ from the typical symbolist poem which seeks through a "medley of metaphors" (Edmund Wilson) to communicate a certain mood, an "état d'âme" which no matter how ineffable is nonetheless coherent and consistent.

What strikes one here, however, is the incongruity of the juxtapositions and the disconcerting shifts of tone. The recluse of "L'Ermite," who has been praying and fasting, apostrophizes a skull in the best *fin de siècle* style—Hamlet's Yorick speech was a great favorite in Paris at the time—when suddenly in his hunger he sees the orbits in the head as holes of a piece of Swiss cheese, and "gruyère" rhymes with "prière." Apollinaire was much too earthy to remain disembodied for long.

"Le Larron" seeks to evoke a mythical pagan land, a composite of ancient civilizations and peoples on whose shore the Christian outsider, the "thief," comes as an intruder. Unlike the vague never-never lands of Maeterlinck's *Pelléas et Mélisande* and Villiers de l'Isle Adam's *Axel*, the mystery here derives from a mass of very precise but recondite allusions based upon an incredible amount of erudition for a twenty-year-old: the Pythagorean peacock, the Tanagra rooster, the stuttering leader, etc. (The glossary in Scott Bates's *Apollinaire* is recommended for readers who wish explanations.) To these are added oracular statements which may or may not make sense:

Le tact est relatif mais la vue est oblongue

After all, "touch *is* relative," as Francis Steegmuller points out, "and sight *is* oblong when you come to think of it: it is the why of the double statement's being made here that is hermetic." Unlike a poet such as Mallarmé, Apollinaire often dissipates the mystery with little explosions of humor, puns, and obscenities, examples of what the French call the *insolite*. The word literally means "unusual" but from Baudelaire down through Ionesco and Beckett has taken on the connotation of "bizarre" or "weirdly unexpected." Apollinaire, as we shall see, was a master of black humor.

Other, shorter poems of this period show the influence of Verlaine: delicate melodious pieces filled with moonbeams, anemones, columbines, and faded gardens, all imbued with gentle melancholy. "Clair de lune" (*Alcools*) is typical, or would be were it not for one little touch which makes it read like a parody of itself. After using one of the most hackneyed examples of synesthesia—mellifluous or honey-flowing moon—Apollinaire adds that the stars can stand "fairly well" for the bees and with this bit of mockery destroys the mood of the metaphor on which the poem is based.

Beginning in 1897 the Dreyfus case was to split France into two camps and by bringing many poets down from the ivory tower into the market place was to contribute heavily to the reaction against symbolism. In 1898 Apollinaire not only declared himself a "Dreyfusard" but expressed his sympathies for the strong anarchist movement then in vogue. One result was a little poem entitled "Au Prolétaire" which its author quite understandably never published. It is frankly bad (unless it be a pastiche) largely because of the clash between the subject matter and a highly precious vocabulary: the smoke from the ugly factories is blown by the "aquilon," the proletarian seamen who have drowned are lulled by "nenias" or Greek funeral dirges. Yet for all its awkwardness the poem reveals that Apollinaire was becoming attuned to a new source of inspiration, the modern industrial city, and like the Belgian poet Verhaeren was trying to combine the urban themes of naturalism with the techniques of symbolism. His visits to Cologne, Düsseldorf, Berlin, and other large cities of Germany and Middle Europe in 1901–2 were to give a more authentic tone to this inspiration.

The German period is one of the richest in Apollinaire's career. He had a truly remarkable gift for immediate assimilation. In Stavelot, where he spent the summer of 1898, he had picked up the Walloon dialect and the local legends of the Ardennes in the space of three months. One of his best short stories, "Que Vlo-ve?" in *L'Hérésiarque et Cie*, comes from this period. Now in the Rhineland, where he served as tutor for a year at Neu-Glück, the family manor of the Vicomtesse de Milhau in the Siebengebirge region and also at Honnef on the Rhine, he discovered a new language and new landscapes, customs, and legends which he made his own. Although he concealed the importance of this sojourn by grouping only nine poems in the "Rhénanes" series in *Alcools*, the fact is that this single year produced almost a third of the works in the collection.

The wide range of subjects and styles suggests that he was intentionally experimenting in new forms and putting the French language to new uses. "La Loreley" is a conscious adaptation of the Brentano and Heine versions. "Nuit rhénane" and "Automne" incorporate elements of German folksongs, and "Les Cloches," although completely original, has the lilt of a *lied*. A number of poems are directly inspired by the landscape: the pine forests ("Les Sapins," "Le Vent nocturne"); the orchards in autumn ("Automne malade"); a herd of cows grazing among the meadow saffron ("Les Colchiques"). Others record little incidents or snapshots caught by the poet: two orthodox Jews arguing on their way to the synagogue in Unkel ("La Synagogue"); children playing in the cemetery of Honnef on All Saints' Day ("Rhénane d'automne"); a prostitute on the Hochstrasse of Cologne ("Marizibill"); housewives chatting in the home of a Honnef winegrower ("Les Femmes"); a boat trip down the Rhine ("Mai"); a visit to a mortuary in Munich ("La Maison des morts"). Only one, "La Tzigane," is directly inspired by a personal, intimate experi-

[15]

ence, a visit made by the poet and his beloved, presumably Annie Playden, the English governess in the household, to a gypsy fortuneteller.

In these pieces Apollinaire was seeking an accommodation between a form of lyricism anchored in reality, whether urban or rural, and the symbolist notion of the poem as an enigma. This involved turning some of the techniques he had tried during his apprenticeship in a new direction and with more subtlety than the purely mechanical juxtapositions of "Au Prolétaire." The imagery becomes more direct. Clearly stated similes replace tenuous metaphors based on synesthesia and other "correspondances," so that the enigmatic quality derives less from the images in themselves than from the arrangement of the lines in which they lie. Two closely related devices predominate: structural ellipsis inherited from the symbolists, and free association, more peculiar to Apollinaire.

The ellipsis is most obviously indicated by double spacing, an invitation to the reader to fill in the blank. The final line of "Nuit rhénane," for instance,

> Mon verre s'est brisé comme un éclat de rire

is set off from the rest of the poem. There is no explanation of why the wine glass breaks; it is up to us to feel the shatter of glass and laughter alike as a sudden catharsis after the intense grief caused by the boatman's song. "Mai" is composed of four stanzas like four separate blocks, the connection among them remaining unexplained because it is one of mood rather than of logical sequence. Within each block as well there are missing links, and by supplying them (in italics) in the first stanza, for example, we destroy the effect:

In May, pretty May *I (?) was* in a boat on the Rhine[.]
Some ladies were looking *down* from the top of the mountain[.]

[16]

And I said to them[, "]You are so pretty[!"(?)] but the boat
  moves on[."(?)]
And they made me wonder[, "]Who caused the river willows
  to weep[?"]

We are not even certain which links to supply, and this ambiguity heightens the tenuous relationship between the rapid
glimpse of the ladies and the sorrow of the willows. The *tem-
pus fugit* theme is a commonplace, and no image could be
more trite than the weeping willow, but the elliptical expression has rejuvenated these elements by creating a fleeting effect
in the form, which harmonizes with the fleeting impressions
from the boat moving rapidly down the Rhine.

Free association is an extreme form of structural ellipsis in
which the link may be hidden or not there at all. In such cases
one is not sure whether a line is mysterious or simply mys-
tifying. In "Les Colchiques" the poisonous flowers resemble
mothers, "daughters of their daughters." Is there a cryptic
connection between an imaginary cyclical process uniting gen-
erations and the circle around the eyes with which the flower
has already been compared? And does this "eternal return"
suggest the fatality of the poet's poisoned love? Or is Apollinaire simply enjoying the repetition of the word "filles" for
its own sake? His fantasy can often be quite gratuitous, and
it would be a mistake to attempt to explicate him as though he
were Mallarmé or Valéry.

In "La Tzigane," on the other hand, there is some free association which effectively intensifies the dominant mood, the
poet's feeling that his love is damned. No obvious connection
exists between love dancing like a bear, the bluebird losing its
feathers, and the beggars losing the *Aves* of their prayers. For
some the sequence may seem as nonsensical as a Mother Goose
rhyme, but for others the deep sense of heaviness and loss is

[17]

as magically and as effortlessly conveyed as by—a Mother Goose rhyme. The same kind of nonsense lines will provide a weird conclusion to the mad dance in a later poem, "Salomé" (*Alcools*), which is worth contrasting with Mallarmé's *Hérodiade* if one wants to appreciate the difference between the master of symbolism and the forerunner of surrealism.

The year in Germany was much more than a training period for the twenty-one-year-old poet. It produced several of those little one-page masterpieces which are among the most loved poems of *Alcools* ("Les Colchiques," "La Tzigane," "Automne malade," etc.), and from it emerged the ingredients of the multidirectional style which in new arrangements and fusions were to form the substance of the major works.

In fact it was only one year later, 1903 (according to his own account), that Apollinaire composed "La Chanson du Mal-Aimé," which many consider his greatest poem and one of the masterpieces of French lyric poetry. Inspired by Annie's rejection of his love in London, where he pursued her after the return from Neu-Glück, it contains all the shades of the poet's ambivalent feelings from deep desire and despair to the most virulent hostility. Much of its power comes from the tension between the opposing principles of continuity and discontinuity in the structure. The octosyllabic five-line stanzas with their *a b a b a* rhyme scheme flow along smoothly, carrying the song of the poet's lost love through the subtly shifting moods. At least *within* each section. The sections themselves, however, stand out like separate, distinct blocks which by their juxtaposition produce a series of unexpected breaks in the flow, as though Stravinsky were driving wedges into Debussy.

The poem opens in the prosaic manner of a short story: "One foggy evening in London . . ." but takes off almost immediately because of the resemblance between the street urchin the solitary narrator meets and his love. The ambiguity of the word "amour" (is it the person or the sentiment or both?) gives a strange, unwholesome quality to the poet's attachment. An obvious analogy, partly visual partly verbal, between the street lined with red bricks and the passage between the Red Sea allows the poet to become the Pharaoh as he pursues the hoodlum. The King of Egypt is the first of a series of legendary monarchs with whom he will associate himself throughout the poem. We know that in London Apollinaire saw the famous Shakespearean actor Beerbohm Tree playing Richard II. Did the "sad stories of the death of kings" spark the poem, not to mention: "Thus play I, in one person, many people . . ."? In any case the device is a particularly effective example of what one critic has called the "plasticity of the self," the constant metamorphoses which Apollinaire undergoes, like a new Proteus.

After protesting candidly to his absent mistress that he really is the King of Egypt *if* she is not his only love (thus developing and destroying the association simultaneously) the poet apparently loses sight of the urchin, who is replaced by the fleeting vision of a drunken woman with a scar on her neck coming out of a pub into the "bleeding fog," at the moment "I recognized the falseness of love itself."

These first five stanzas transform the modern city into a phantasmagoria more eerie than sordid in which the narrator becomes the suffering hero of some strange legend, unknown because it is new. With these several lines Apollinaire has brought us much closer to the streets of Breton's *Nadja* and Aragon's *Paysan de Paris* than to the castles of *Axel* and *Pelléas et Mélisande*.

Beginning with the sixth stanza a sharp break in the narration evokes the happy return of the mythical kings, Ulysses and Dushyanta, to their faithful wives. These two vignettes create a change in tone which serves to intensify by contrast the poet's grief at the faithlessness of his own beloved. The ensuing stanzas flow smoothly on the "beautiful ship" of the poet's memory backwards in time to the dawn of his love affair, leading to an aubade, the first of three interludes set apart typographically with their titles as poems within the poem.

Rarely has a writer borrowed from himself so much as Apollinaire. The majority of the poems in *Alcools* and many in *Calligrammes* contain individual lines, stanzas, or whole sections removed from their original position and placed in different surroundings. If this be "collage," as it is often called, Apollinaire was practicing it long before Braque and Picasso. In "La Chanson du Mal-Aimé" we know from their manuscripts that the Reply of the Zaporogian Cossacks and the section on Shakuntala, the wife of Dushyanta, were composed earlier as separate pieces. The same may well be true of the Aubade, and even for the readers ignorant of such bits of scholarly evidence the interludes and the other equally autonomous groups of stanzas make for a quiltlike pattern in the poem as a whole.

The jubilant neoclassical tone of the Aubade gives way immediately to a mood of despondency. The poet knows the pagan gods have died, as have indeed the Christian god and Love itself; the only idols he can adore are the memories of his love. He thus remains faithful to something defunct, like the wife of King Mausolus. The thought that he is unable to free himself from this empty adoration exasperates him so intensely that some kind of an explosion is bound to follow, and we come to the "Reply of the Zaporogian Cossacks to the Sultan of

Constantinople," certainly one of the most unexpected ("insolite") fragments that one can hope to find in any love poem. The Cossacks, who have just received an ultimatum to surrender to the Mohammedan monarch, compose with a burst of mirthless laughter their foul-mouthed reply. For them the laugh is an act of defiance, but for the poet-lover it is a purge for his grief and his mortification at finding himself the victim of a passionate, impossible attachment. And indirectly through a kind of poetic logic the impassive young Puritan girl who inspired the poem is splattered by the most ungallant ribaldry.

Apollinaire revels in contrasts. One of the most horrendously sadistic orgies in his pornographic novel, *Les Onze Mille Verges*, is followed by a description of a placid Rhineland scene before dawn, a real gem of pastoral writing. Similarly the beautifully mysterious stanza which comes after the Cossacks' Reply and which constitutes a refrain by its repetition elsewhere in the poem:

Voie lactée ô soeur lumineuse . . .

evokes the quiescence of the poet's grief after the catharsis. There follows a long section of fourteen stanzas setting forth the subtle modulations of the emotions of the Mal-Aimé—resignation, nostalgia, self-pity, morbid longing—and leading to the third interlude, "The Seven Swords" of the poet's melancholy. Adapting to his own purposes the symbolism of the Madonna of the Seven Sorrows and the Seven Swords of the tarot cards, Apollinaire has created a highly original and hermetic projection of the facets and phases of his love. Numerous exegeses astrological, philological, and erotological have sought to pierce the mysteries of these lines. Perhaps the most satisfying approach is simply to imagine that the seven stanzas were penned by some anonymous medieval bard who happened to have lived in the twentieth century under the name of Guillaume Apollinaire.

For all its hermeticism "The Seven Swords" serves to objectify the sorrow of the poet-lover and thus prepare the resolution of the "Chanson." Before reaching the conclusion, however, we pass through a block of stanzas which because of its parallel position just inside the gates of the poem forms a pathetic contrast with the section on the happy monarchs, Ulysses and Dushyanta. It presents the ill-starred brothers Ludwig and Otto of Bavaria, both mad, and particularly the love-lorn Ludwig who drowned himself in a lake

Près d'un château sans châtelaine.

This final paroxysm of grief is perhaps the most intense in the entire poem with its suggestion for the Mal-Aimé that in suicide lies the only solution.

The parallelism is even neater between the concluding five-stanza section and its counterpart of equal length at the beginning. In this "tale of two cities" the June sun, the noisy street, and the cafés of Paris offset the fog and the weird, unwholesome silence of London. The poet no longer has the heart to die. In the frank, authentic atmosphere of his own city he recognizes beyond a doubt that his love has no future, no ambiguous hopes. The sun, which becomes a flaming lyre burning his aching fingers, symbolizes the poet's need, his decision (as with the symbolists and Proust) to convert the heart-rending experience through which he has passed, and which we have witnessed all along the way, into a work of art, the very one that he has just written and that we have just read. The final lines repeat emphatically an earlier stanza declaring our hero's knowledge of the secrets of song: "I who know . . . songs for the sirens." Later on Apollinaire was to write that "those who are reasonable, that is to say the poets, profit from their sufferings in love by singing them." This does not necessarily imply, however, an absolute victory, as the symbolists would imagine, of "Art" over "Life." "Song" is a more modest word; the grief is still there, and the most we dare say is simply that Kostrowitzky has become Apollinaire.

One has only to recall the single, fixed décor of the most celebrated French love poem of the nineteenth century, Lamartine's "Le Lac," to appreciate the tremendous diversity of material in "La Chanson du Mal-Aimé." Disparate blocks of imagination jostle each other between the two terminal points which pin down the poem in reality. Discontinuity of course is a risky technique which can easily become the enemy of coherence. The problem for Apollinaire was to create an effect of disorder reflecting the turbulence of the poet-lover's distraught soul while imposing enough order to make the poem aesthetically valid. Hence the necessity for a compromise with the devices of continuity: the regular verse form, the more or less symmetrical architecture (avoiding at all costs the coldly mathematical), the transitional stanzas uniting certain but by no means all of the sections. Thanks to these compromises the lyric sentiment is at once multifaceted and single. Projected into the vastness of history and legend it retains at the same time all the intimacy of the subjective self. Much of the power of "La Chanson du Mal-Aimé" derives from the delicate balance it achieves between "Order" and "Adventure," the Apollonian and the Dionysian.

"L'Emigrant de Landor Road" (*Alcools*), which dates from the same period (1904–5), commemorates—with a transposition of the sexes—Annie's departure from her home on Landor Road for the United States in order to escape the importunities of "Kostro." Its rich patchwork structure foreshadows the

[23]

1907–8 period when structural ellipses and free association based on the principle of discontinuity will be most fully developed and incorporated in a new aesthetic.

Meanwhile Apollinaire passed through a period of deep discouragement and sterility. Was it a kind of "season in Hell"? We have little information on his state of mind at this time. The year 1906 is almost a complete blank. In reply to an interview in September he said, "I have no significant work and I regret it." (The manuscript of "La Chanson du Mal-Aimé" was lying in the desk drawer of the editor of *Le Mercure de France*, waiting to be discovered three years later.) "Cortège," which seems to date at least in part from this moment, reveals the poet's anguished search for his identity, the relationship of his "I" to the rest of the universe, and concludes with a eulogy of the past as opposed to the "colorless" future.

In 1908 Apollinaire emerged with the publication of a surrealist text, "Onirocritique" (*Il y a*), and two major poems, "Le Brasier" and "Fiançailles" (*Alcools*), which announce the discovery of a new poetic language. The rough draft of "Les Fiançailles" in particular and of course the text itself constitute our main source of knowledge of the crisis he had just gone through. During the war he wrote that he considered this poem along with "Le Brasier" as his best work. Posterity has not confirmed this judgment, but "Les Fiançailles" is probably the most important work for his development, his "Demoiselles d'Avignon," as it were. In fact it is dedicated to Picasso and was conceived at roughly the same time as the painting. For those who like to call Apollinaire a "cubist poet" it is tempting to imagine the two men working out their new aesthetic together.

A more verifiable influence is that of the neo-symbolist *Phalange* group with which Apollinaire began collaborating in

1907 and which was engaged in a reevaluation of Mallarmé's poetics with its concept of the poem as an autonomous object subject to a multiplicity of interpretations. Rimbaud too must have played a formative role—"Onirocritique" could hardly have been written without the *Illuminations*—but external evidence is lacking. Apollinaire was always strangely silent about Rimbaud.

In any case, if neo-symbolism and nascent cubism were the accoucheurs of "Les Fiançailles," the birth pangs were Apollinaire's own. It is the first poem in which he confides so openly about his ecstasies and sufferings as a poet. He tells of his grandiose projects as a youth, and in fact the first two of the nine sections are fragments from two long 1902 poems, one pastoral, one urban, like exhibits on display exemplifying two distinct styles which the poet now intends to fuse. He tells how he sought for absolute purity but realizes now that perfection lies in the moment, that poetry is a state of mind rather than a work. He confesses the "torments" of silence that he has just suffered. At times he sees himself as a divine stellar force: it is toward *his* eyes that Icarus rises. Then again he glimpses only his mortal self with death rushing upon him "like a hurricane." He proclaims his omniscience—only to ask forgiveness for his ignorance. The single constant in these fluctuations seems to be his love, a love so all-inclusive that it must embrace the totality of life.

"Les Fiançailles" ends triumphantly with a phoenixlike regeneration of the poet's spirit. More specifically—and here perhaps lies the key to an understanding of this very obscure poem—it is his "incertitude" that is reborn out of its own ashes. In this one word Apollinaire sums up all the oscillations and indecisions of his mercurial character which were constantly threatening to make a jumble of inconsistencies of his rootless existence. "Les Fiançailles" is thus the dramatization of a decision, not the decision to choose from among the conflicting forces within him, since this would mean suppressing others—and on what basis could the choice be made?—but rather the decison to embrace them all by fully recognizing their simultaneous existence. Of "incertitude" itself he would make a principle and a source of plenitude, bringing his life and his poetry into focus as through a single lens.

Rereading the poem with this in mind one discovers that its very style illustrates this sense of totality. Whether one calls this "cubism" or more accurately "simultanism" (with a broader connotation than that of the 1912 school which Apollinaire himself attempted to incorporate in his term "orphism") it consists of the interlocking of opposites in new syntheses through the use of words and images with multiple meanings placed in discontinuous lines and sections in an effort to nullify the flow of time and thus achieve an effect of ambivalent immediacy.

The trouble with "Les Fiançailles" is its very excess of riches. Intoxicated by this revelation the author has packed the poem with a bewildering profusion of ambiguities, fused dichotomies, shifting images with shifting meanings, collages that only he can recognize, and secret allusions to which he holds the keys. Although "Le Brasier" grew out of the same drafts it is more coherent because, as the title indicates, it centers upon the single element of fire. One of the main traits of Apollinaire's imagery in general is its volatility. Objects visually perceived and simple in themselves constantly melt into one another, a bit like the underlying phallic motif on the amphorae and frescoes of ancient Knossos which appears alternately as a fleur-de-lys, a torso with arms akimbo, a neck with two bosoms, an octopus head, a butterfly. Whole chains can be established in Apollinaire: leaf to hand to flame to heart; shadow to snake to flame to sun to neck. Like Michelangelo, who believed that moving figures should be given the form of flames, he apparently realized around 1908 that the image of fire is paramount because it connects and contains the others. Although its presence in "Les Fiançailles" is more diffuse than in "Le Brasier" it becomes in both poems the all-embracing symbol of poetic inspiration in general, of the poetic rebirth of 1908 in particular, and of the multiplicity-into-unity principle upon which it is based. Later on in *Les Peintres cubistes* Apollinaire was to sum up the genius of Picasso in two words: "enormous flame."

The note of hope and affirmation at the end of "Les Fiançailles" persists in the 1909 poems: "Poème lu au mariage d'André Salmon," "1909," and especially "Vendémiaire" (*Alcools*). The uninterrupted ebulliency of the last work makes it perhaps the most Dionysian piece that Apollinaire wrote. Few French writers—one thinks of Rabelais, Hugo, Claudel—have reached such sustained dithyrambic intensity. Apollinaire turns his visionary power outwards upon the modern cities, transfiguring those of France, Europe, and the world into great vats of intoxicating wine. And it is the poet himself who drinks it all, for he is "the throat of Paris," the city supreme.

"Le Voyageur," another offshoot of the 1908 discoveries, turns the techniques of simultaneity inward upon the poet's deep solitude, which it relates to his sense of the instability, the constant flux of existence. The two opening alexandrine lines, separated like two monostichs, announce the dual theme:

Ouvrez-moi cette porte où je frappe en pleurant

La vie est variable aussi bien que l'Euripe

The first line has all the dramatic urgency of an anguished

[27]

cry emerging from nowhere. The second, which alludes to a strait in Greece famous for its surging currents and counter-currents, reads like an aphorism, a detached observation. The two together fuse the subjective and the objective views of the poet-traveler's condition. They also announce the form of the poem, which will consist of a montage of isolated and uncertain recollections and free associations surging forth helter-skelter from the memory of the poet who may be ad-dressing an unnamed interlocutor or more probably himself. The reader who tries to find a sequence in the fragments of the poem would do well to remember the observation of T. S. Eliot (in *The Use of Poetry and the Use of Criticism*):

Why, for all of us, out of all that we have heard, seen, felt, in a lifetime, do certain images recur, charged with emotion, rather than others? The song of one bird, the leap of one fish, at a par-ticular place and time, the scent of one flower, an old woman on a German mountain path, six ruffians seen through an open win-dow playing cards at night at a small French railway junction where there was a watermill; such memories may have symbolic value, but of what we cannot tell, for they come to represent the depths of feeling into which we cannot peer.

Fragments of remembered reality fall in alongside strange dreamlike scenes, such as the recurrent picture of the two sail-ors. There seems to be no rigorous necessity in the selection and arrangement of the "old photos." Apollinaire might have chosen others, but these were simply the ones which tumbled out. The one section which seems least automatic, consisting as it does of four highly polished alexandrine quatrains, is actu-ally a kind of recollection in itself, an old manuscript of Apol-linaire which he has inserted as a private piece of collage. It is far from gratuitous, however. The silent, bearded shadows passing across a mountain, holding their lances before them, seem to emerge from the dim, mythical past of a Jungian mem-

[28]

ory. Like the allusions to the monarchs in "La Chanson du Mal-Aimé" these lines cause the poem to open out into a mysterious new perspective in time.

The poem ends as it began. Nothing is resolved, but the two lines of the opening, enriched now by all the evocations within, restate with greater intensity the same sense of solitude and instability and even suggest as well the absurdity of this condition. For the effect of incoherence in the form reflects the meaningless incoherence, the "deadendedness" of life. Less ambitious—one is almost tempted to say less pretentious—than the other major poems of the period, "Le Voyageur" is undoubtedly one of the most authentic and deeply moving poems in *Alcools*. If one were to define the emotion it conveys it would perhaps not be an exaggeration to call it a mixture of pity and terror.

The high-reaching revelations of "Les Fiançailles" did not preclude the composing of little poems and songs. From 1908 to 1912 Apollinaire wrote quite a few which it would be a great mistake to consider as mere divertissements. The original version of *Le Bestiaire* first appeared in 1908 between the publication dates of "Le Brasier" and "Les Fiançailles." (It came out in book form with woodcuts by Dufy in 1911.) The sprightly humor of these well-chiseled four- and five-line pieces often veils some very complex sentiments. The "incertitude" of the crayfish, for example, is the same as that of the bird in "Les Fiançailles."

Two of the best short poems in *Alcools* were inspired by the unhappy end of the liaison with Marie Laurencin in 1912: "Le Pont Mirabeau," the famous anthology selection, and "Cors de chasse." The second illustrates more richly the 1908 aesthetic. The opening line:

> Notre histoire est noble et tragique

[29]

is ambiguous enough to refer to an entire people and inspire Archibald MacLeish's "Men," beginning:

> Our history is grave noble and tragic

or to a private love affair. The theme of tragic ineluctability evoked in this first stanza and the poisonous effects of Thomas de Quincey's opium in the second recall a similar relationship in "Les Colchiques," with this difference, however, that in the Rhineland poem the mothers, "daughters of their daughters," are compared to the poisonous flower in an explicit simile joined by "comme," whereas in "Cors de chasse" the structural ellipsis between the two stanzas obliges the reader to make the associative leap. He thus experiences more immediately the sense of the poisonous inevitability of love, its predestined permanence. The very moment, however, that he grasps this feeling he reads that all is ephemeral:

> Passons passons puisque tout passe

and that even memories die:

> Les souvenirs sont cors de chasse
> Dont meurt le bruit parmi le vent

Thanks to the omission of adversative conjunctions the reader shares with the poet the full impact of the very Heraclitean dialectic of permanence and flow. "Le Pont Mirabeau" presents essentially the same theme, but through the use of ellipsis "Cors de chasse" develops it more subtly, and the concluding couplet, isolated from the rest, becomes, as Marie-Jeanne Durry points out in her study of *Alcools*, the ultimate, quintessential expression after Vigny, Baudelaire, Verlaine, and Laforgue of the hunting horn–memory motif in French poetry.

The loss of Marie Laurencin is only one contributing factor to the inspiration underlying "Zone." This work was long considered most important as Apollinaire's manifesto of modernism. Although "Zone" was the last poem to be composed for *Alcools*, its position at the beginning of the volume with its categorical statement of the opening line:

A la fin tu es las de ce monde ancien

seems to announce an abrupt change of direction in 1913, the decision, like that of Marinetti's futurists, to sing of the dynamism of the twentieth-century world. The first twenty-four lines, which evoke the beauty of the industrial age, confirm this impression, as will a number of the poems composed thereafter, most of which appeared in Apollinaire's avant-garde magazine, *Les Soirées de Paris*. Today most of us would be inclined to agree with Hart Crane, who wrote bluntly in a letter, "All this talk from Matty [Matthew Josephson] on Apollinaire about being gay and *so* distressingly and painfully delighted about the telegraph, the locomotive, the automat, the wireless, the street cars and electric lamp posts, annoys me." Actually, as we have seen, Apollinaire had already developed a more profoundly modern sensibility and style long before, and if "Zone" still has a strong appeal more than a half-century later as one of the major poems of *Alcools*, the reasons are completely different.

It is perhaps the masterpiece of what one might call Apollinaire's peripatetic poetry (in the literal sense of the word). He loved to walk. To a collection of essays on Paris he gave the title *Le Flâneur des deux rives*, and the action of his short stories often grows out of a strange encounter on a city street, as in "Le Passant de Prague" (*L'Hérésiarque et Cie*). Whether on the open road or the open street it is as a wanderer, usually alone, that the poet or a *persona* he creates sets the scene in such diverse poems of *Alcools* as "La Maison des morts,"

[31]

"Marizibill," "Rhénane d'automne," "Mai," "La Chanson du Mal-Aimé," "L'Emigrant de Landor Road," "Annie," "Rose-monde," "Cortège," "Les Fiançailles" (Parts II, VII, VIII), "Le Voyageur," "Marie," and "Vendémiaire." And the practice will continue in *Calligrammes* with such "poèmes-promenades" as "Le Musicien de Saint-Merry" and "Un Fantôme de nuées."

Apollinaire's penchant for this type comes primarily from his "disponibilité," that feeling of openness to whatever encounter the moving landscape might provide. Like the surrealists after him he depended upon fortuitous occurrences to trigger his imagination. In "Lettre-Océan" (*Calligrammes*) he writes:

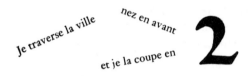

It is the immediate contact between the external scene and the poet's "nose" as an antenna that sets the poem going.

"Zone" is particularly successful as a "poème-promenade" because the "peripatetic" motion governs the form throughout. The title suggests both the Parisian term for the suburbs sur-rounding the city and etymologically the somewhat beltlike or circular direction of the walk, which continues from one morning to the next, interrupted by several stops (the Gare Saint-Lazare, a bar, a restaurant, a brothel) before the poet returns at sunrise to his apartment in the suburb of Auteuil. The correlation between the ever increasing fatigue of the walk and the despondency of the poet is implied all along.

Within this framework, which shows the real city unfolding

before him, the poet introduces a series of memories from the various stages of his past life, and it soon becomes apparent that he is endeavoring to reconcile present and past time on a single plane or more precisely to reconcile his conflicting feelings toward two sets of opposites in time. The opening lines seek to proclaim enthusiastically the rejection of the past in its obvious connotation of "old" in favor of the present as "new." But the ratio is not so simple. Line 25:

Voilà la jeune rue et tu n'es encore qu'un petit enfant

introduces a sudden switch as in a chiasmus. Newness becomes associated with the past, the poet's childhood, as he recalls his religious fervor at the Collège Saint-Charles; and the naïve image of Jesus as an aviator, along with the imaginary parade of the birds which welcome the "flying machine," simply manifests a desperate effort to impose the enchantment of his boyhood faith upon the modern world of today. The attempt fails, and the sections beginning with the line:

Maintenant tu marches dans Paris tout seul parmi la foule

suggest the other pair of the reversed ratio. The present about him has lost all its freshness, and the poet finds himself overwhelmed by his despondency. As he continues his walk he desperately attempts once more to resuscitate his past in a series of rapid flashbacks beginning with:

Maintenant tu es au bord de la Méditerranée

all moved into the present tense. Gradually, however, the magic of the memories pales, and nothing is left at the end but the pitiful sordidness of the actual city with its emigrants and prostitutes:

Tu regardes les yeux pleins de larmes ces pauvres émigrants

The poet gradually makes his way home to sleep among the only remnants of his lost faith, the "fetishes from Oceania and Guinea . . . the inferior Christs of dark hopes." Daybreak—the hour for guillotinings in France—calls up through free association the final sinister image of the rising sun as a severed neck:

Soleil cou coupé

(The terse dissonance of this line made it famous among the surrealists, and the revolutionary Negro poet Aimé Césaire has used it as the title of one of his principal volumes.)

As an attempt to deal with the contradictions implicit in the concept of time, "Zone" is the poetic counterpart in miniature of a novel which began to appear the same year: *A la recherche du temps perdu*. Both seek to surpass the division between past and present in a new synthesis which, thanks to memory, would resurrect "lost time" in all its resplendence. Unlike Proust, Apollinaire sought the palingenesis through religious faith, which makes the confession of his failure all the more poignant. His compassion for the outcasts toward the end of the poem is certainly a Christian virtue, but Faith and Hope have gone. Only Charity remains.

Its stark ending did not prevent "Zone" from becoming the great avant-garde banner of the "Counter-Decadence," and it is usually cited as the "cubist" poem par excellence. No doubt it produces a fragmented, multidimensional effect through such devices as the telescoping of syntax, the almost exclusive use of the present tense, the rapid shifting of personal pronouns, the abrupt changes of locale, and the suppression of connectives and of course of punctuation. As we have seen, however, its basic structure remains sequential rather than simultaneous. If cubism is indeed a "sum of destructions" as Picasso claimed, in the sense that the fragmented elements of reality are re-arranged so as to create a state of tension between the opposing forces of unity and multiplicity, then both the structure and the greater degree of polyvalence in "Les Fiançailles" and "Le Voyageur" make them more truly "cubist" than "Zone," which for all its zigzags flows along in time like "La Chanson du Mal-Aimé."

The reputation of "Zone" as a cubist poem stems in part from its prepublication appearance in the newly founded *Soirées de Paris*. Right up to the outbreak of World War I this magazine was one of the principal mouthpieces for the new painting, with which Apollinaire found himself more feverishly involved than at any other time. Almost half the entire output of his art criticism dates from this two-and-a-half-year period. He visited scores of galleries, lectured at the important cubist "Section d'or" exhibit, visited England with Picabia, went to Berlin with Delaunay to lecture on modern painting, published *Les Peintres cubistes*, issued a manifesto on futurism, wrote about the New York Armory Show, and introduced Chagall, de Chirico, Archipenko, and numerous other unknown artists to the Parisian public.

A mere glance at the first section of *Calligrammes* shows how the poems of this period were affected. Lyricism gives way to experimentation, and most of the experiments are designed to bring poetry closer to painting. "Les Fenêtres," composed for the catalogue of a Delaunay exhibit, and "A travers l'Europe," inspired by a visit to Chagall's studio, seek to evoke with words the spirit or style of a painter; and in the posthumous works one finds pieces on Picasso, Rousseau, Picabia, Survage, Lagut, *et al.* The first calligrams appeared in *Les Soirées de Paris*, accompanied by a fellow critic's explanation that they oblige our mind to understand "synthetico-ideographically" instead of "analytico-discursively." The outbreak of the war prevented Apollinaire from carrying out his plan to publish them separately under the title *Moi aussi je suis peintre.*

In general the 1912–14 poems push the cubist principle of fragmentation to the extreme. The "blocks" become shorter, the images and statements more heterogeneous. Notations replace complete sentences. Free, blank verse becomes the rule. Like the futurist *parole in libertà* the lines, if not always the actual words, have declared their independence. Has coherence become taboo? Is the reader who earnestly seeks some elusive "objective correlative" making a fool of himself? That depends upon the poem. In some, no doubt, chance plays the dominant role. The "poèmes-conversations" like "Lundi rue Christine" record the haphazard flow of real scraps of conversation around the pivotal point of the poet. In "Liens," on the other hand, the diverse images all relate to the theme of bonds or ties announced by the title, and the poem's coherence derives from the harmonious fusion of the techniques of simultanism in the form and the ambivalent feelings toward interdependence which they express. With "Arbre" one can't be sure. Is the statement toward the end:

L'univers se plaint par ta voix

the thematic magnet which attracts all the disparate lines, or do they remain scattered? The poem seems to hover between the cubist principle of composition and the destructive anarchy of Dada. Its publication in the dadaists' first magazine, *Le Cabaret Voltaire*, in 1916 confirms that they themselves claimed the poem as their own.

Their selection of a prewar poem by Apollinaire further suggests that by August, 1914, he had in effect reached the limits of his experimentation. The war poetry, which constitutes about three-fourths of *Calligrammes*, introduces a completely new décor, but the techniques, for all their regroupings, are familiar. The peacetime imagery is replaced by trenches, barbed wire, cannon, and hand grenades, but the analogies are as volatile as before, a German shell, for example, becoming in turn a woman's breast, a rose, a heart, a star.

If the same techniques persist it is simply that Apollinaire himself did not change.

Incertitude ô mes délices

True to himself Apollinaire sensed that every attitude generates its own contradiction and that in the horror of war lies its very fascination. In his poetry from 1914 to 1918 ambivalence was to go on wearing the garb of simultanism.

Critics often accuse him of prettifying war, of watching a battle as jubilantly as a July 14 fireworks display; and they quote the famous line:

Ah Dieu! que la guerre est jolie ("L'Adieu du cavalier")

Only out of context, however, can the line be taken literally, for the soldier who utters it is immediately killed! Its true meaning was grasped by those who used it recently as the title for the Paris production of the London musical *Oh! What a Lovely War*. Apollinaire's experiences at the front were to intensify his black humor. From his youth he had felt the influence of Alfred Jarry, but it was not until 1915 that he made a direct reference to Ubu, calling the war, in a rather bad pun, "Obus-Roi." Like Jarry he mingles farce and fury, turning the tragic inside out, and by making death a subject for laughter conveys more freshly all its horror. Face to face with death he can affect the most insensitive cheerfulness, a kind of amused detachment, or a puckish smile. He can make the most abrupt

[37]

leaps from the anguished, heavyhearted self within him, who feels deeply the tragedy of man's condition, to himself as *persona*, detached, inhuman, an "image d'Epinal" soldier, "Guy au galop," a stranger as mysterious and alarming as the stylized characters of a Guignol theater. André Breton has recalled the sound of Apollinaire's laughter as he heard it shortly before the poet's death. "It made the same noise as a first burst of hailstones on a window pane." The implication is that this laugh had nothing contagious about it; it caused no merriment but a shudder, a feeling of malaise. Was it not a sudden outburst of the more unfeeling, destructive side of the poet's nature? The only difference between Apollinaire and his "hypocrite lecteur" was that he fully recognized the presence of this fact and expressed it freely.

The war also sharpened his perception of the mysterious links between death and Eros. "The terrible, warlike god of love," he writes. Through the hundred-odd poems addressed from the front to "Lou" and to Madeleine (published posthumously in *Ombre de mon amour* and *Tendre comme le souvenir*) there runs a current of violent sensuality which the occasionally modified versions selected for *Calligrammes* only partially reveal. The privations of trench life and the constant presence of death acerbate the poet's desires to a point where he often fuses in richly ambiguous imagery the instruments of devastation and those of propagation, turning no-man's-land into a vast erogenous zone. The analogies work both ways. A white trench (Apollinaire fought on the chalky soil of Champagne) becomes a deathly-pale nymphomaniac enticing her soldier-lovers ("La Tranchée" in *Tendre comme le souvenir*, abridged in "Chant d'honneur," *Calligrammes*). In "Chef de section" (*Calligrammes*), as the soldier stands poised, watch in hand, waiting to give the signal for an attack, his beloved becomes the enemy and his mouth a Gehenna full of flames.

Because of its restraint and concision "Fête" in *Calligrammes* is perhaps the masterpiece of this genre. It consists of a subtly iridescent play between the triple analogy of bursting shell, rose, and bosom, and the twofold sentiment uniting fear of death with erotic desire.

On March 17, 1916, as Apollinaire was sitting in the trench reading the *Mercure de France*, a shell fragment pierced his helmet and entered the right temple. The convalescence after the trepanation was slow, and it was not until August that he began to frequent the cafés of Montparnasse and the Café de Flore close by his apartment on the Boulevard Saint-Germain. In a final letter to Madeleine in November he confesses his lassitude and admits he has changed. Actually the same old incertitude is there, but for the next two years, which are like a reprieve from death, it will oscillate mainly along the axis between avant-gardism and conservatism, two poles which Apollinaire will not always manage to synthesize.

In his appearance at least he succeeded, as he sat chatting with left-bank dadaists in his horizon blue uniform and the croix de guerre, which appears in both the Picasso and Modigliani portraits. It was this same uniform at the premiere of the Cocteau-Satie-Picasso-Massine ballet *Parade* in 1917 that saved the authors from the fists of a scandalized audience. Apollinaire's patriotism instilled in him the obligation to preach the good old virtues of French classicism: honor, duty, and above all order. The man who only four years earlier had issued his revolutionary manifesto, *L'Antitradition futuriste*, now claimed prudently in his lecture on the New Spirit that "as a rule you will not find in France those *parole in libertà* of the Italian and Russian futurists who have pushed the new spirit too far; for France abhors disorder." Shortly before his death Apollinaire confided to Picasso that he was writing verse "more in line with your own preoccupations of the moment.

[39]

I am trying to renew my poetic tone but within the classical rhythm." (Picasso was in fact embarking on what has been called his "classico-expressionist" style.) And in the same letter he adds: "What could be newer today, more modern, more unadorned and richer than Pascal? You enjoy him too, I believe, and rightly so." Beneath all the farcical chaos of *Les Mamelles de Tirésias* lies a comic plot in the best seventeenth-century manner. Like Monsieur Jourdain in Molière's *Bourgeois gentilhomme* Thérèse wants to become what she is not, in her case a feminist. It doesn't take her long, however, after changing into Tiresias to realize that she is better off as a woman, and the metamorphosis back to Thérèse makes her a good housewife ready to produce progeniture for the *patrie*. *Castigo ridendo mores.*

"Kostro," it seems, has finally taken root—in the Age of Louis XIV! Yet his biographers inevitably entitle the 1916–18 period "L'Esprit nouveau," and there is ample evidence to show that he was still out in front of the avant-garde. He states, for example, that the New Spirit seeks to "explore every field that can provide literary material for the exaltation of life in whatever form it occurs." His thirst for spiritual ubiquity remains as strong as ever, but he is less concerned with the techniques of simultanism in poetry alone than with the discovery of new media and sources in all the arts. The bars are down. So long as it extends the range of expression any means is acceptable. "We want new sounds new sounds new sounds," he exclaims in "La Victoire" (*Calligrammes*) and proposes consonants without vowels, prolonged nasals, tongue clicking, finger snapping, drumlike beats on the cheek, imitations of a spinning top. In 1917 he announces the birth of a new art, the "tactile art" based on surprising combinations of stickiness, elasticity, softness, the oily, the silky, the velvety. More serious are his hopes for the phonograph and the cinema, "vaster than the plain art of words," and he predicts the day when they will replace printing, giving poets a freedom hitherto unknown.

Meanwhile he chides the poet of today for his "crawling imagination," long since outdistanced by the scientists, and exhorts him to dig into his unconscious for new riches and to focus his imagination on the everyday event: "The dropping of a handkerchief can be the lever with which he will lift up a whole universe." This notion of the infinite sources of inspiration is most beautifully expressed in "La Jolie Rousse," where Apollinaire addresses the traditionalists in the name of the avant-garde:

> Nous voulons vous donner de vastes et d'étranges domaines
> Où le mystère en fleurs s'offre à qui veut le cueillir
> Mille phantasmes impondérables
> Auxquels il faut donner de la réalité

Above all Apollinaire campaigns for works which would orchestrate the various arts on a vaster, more modern plane than the Wagnerian *Gesamtkunstwerk* which had influenced the symbolists. *Parade* delighted him for this very reason since Cocteau's script, Satie's music, Picasso's sets and costumes, and Massine's choreography fused the elements of contemporary reality: music hall motifs, skyscrapers, typewriters, American ragtime, in one "total" scenic poem. To characterize this amalgamation, in his program notes for the premiere Apollinaire coined a new word: surrealism. A month later (June, 1917) the same concept of total theater is implicit in his second use of the word as the subtitle ("drame surréaliste") of *Les Mamelles de Tirésies*, for the prologue stresses that the collaboration of the arts ("sounds gestures movements masses color") produces not the imitation of a "slice of life" but life itself in its totality.

When the surrealists appropriated the word seven years later they stripped it of both its theatrical and its aesthetic connotations, substituting (but without giving credit) Apollinaire's notion of the "automatic life," as Roger Shattuck has called it, the belief, that is, that one should act "in total response to one's deepest nature without rejecting the contradictions or paradoxes inherent in that nature."

Apollinaire was so feverishly involved in other fields during his last two years that his poetry suffers. *Calligrammes* includes only four pieces written after the convalescence. *Vitam impendere amori* and a handful of other pieces published posthumously complete the entire output. Yet these few works give a truer picture of the poet's complex "état d'âme" than the fictional, dramatic, and critical writing. If he had neatly trimmed his thought to the simple dualities of "Order" and "Adventure" how can one explain the dejected conclusion of "La Jolie Rousse" ("Ayez pitié de moi")? What is the "secret misfortune" in "Tristesse d'une étoile," the "heavy secret" of *Vitam impendere amore*, the recurrent theme of suffering in "Les Collines"? First it is to be noted that these poems retain the rich polyvalence Apollinaire discovered a decade earlier with "Les Fiançailles." The flame returns as the all-inclusive image: in fact in the "New Spirit" lecture he explicitly uses it as the symbol of polyvalence in speaking of "the immense unknown where the joyous fires of multiple meanings blaze forth."

In "La Jolie Rousse" the flame not only succeeds in fusing Order and Adventure in a single entity—"La Raison ardente" (since "ardent" retains from its old French root *ardre* the original meaning of "burning")—but further associates this entity with the red hair of the beloved (Jacqueline), the hot summer (the poet's maturity), the sun (the force which generates ardor), and a lightning flash which endures (the continuity of his inspiration). At this point, however, a dissonant note is introduced through the image of flames in withering roses, which suggests the connection between fire and death. This is the final image that leads directly to the dejected conclusion of the poem. In "Tristesse d'une étoile" the same adjective *ardente* modifies the secret "suffering" which the poet carries within him, like the flaming body of the glowworm, like France within the heart of the soldier, like pollen within the heart of the lily. Here we go a step further since the similes make it clear that the suffering is simultaneously destructive and regenerative, but its exact nature remains a mystery. Perhaps "Les Collines" will give an inkling.

This poem has much the same visionary tone as "Les Fiançailles" and "Le Brasier," with the poet not only seeing himself as an omniscient celestial force endowed with the gift of prophecy but predicting in addition the divinization of mankind. Yet this messianic optimism is offset by the insistence that the future will be a time of deep suffering and indeed that suffering, like the unconscious, will become a subject for scientific study. This theme is so emphatic that it strikes one less as a prediction than as a vast projection of the poet's own obsessive "secret" and introduces a disquieting contradiction to the ebullient hopes. The flame is particularly effective in underlining this ambivalence. At the beginning of the poem two airplanes are fighting. One is the poet's youth, the other the future. When we read: "Where has my youth fallen?" we understand which plane has won the battle, but how then do we interpret the line:

Tu vois que flambe l'avenir

except as an expression of the poet's contradictory feelings

[43]

toward the future which is flaming gloriously and tragically at the same time? Similarly in the concluding stanza the secret of life itself is summed up in the line:

Tout n'est qu'une flamme rapide

which in the context cannot be read with this or that connotation of "flame" in mind but with its contradictory meanings fused.

"La Jolie Rousse," like "Le Brasier," derives its coherence from the element of fire, but in "Les Collines," as in "Les Fiançailles," this element remains more diffuse, mingling with numerous other images in one of the most volatile poems Apollinaire wrote. The rapidity of the metamorphoses which the poet presents or undergoes builds up to such a frenetic, desperate pitch that it may at last give us a clue to the nature of his secret torment. "Les Collines" is a fine example of surrealism insofar as it is composed of a vertiginous sequence of images, each one of which, if we may apply a remark of Aragon, "obliges you at each moment to change your view of the entire Universe." Like Apollinaire, surrealism sought to convey to modern man, outside the perimeter of religion, a feeling of transcendency, but as Yves Bonnefoy has pointed out, surrealism lived on a contradiction, which it refused to admit, between its desire for participation in the sacred and "its secret love of nothingness."

Did Apollinaire admit such a contradiction? Not in so many words. Yet the nihilistic undertone which we have already discerned in "Le Voyageur" and "Zone" recurs in "Les Collines," particularly in an arresting image which describes the act of going back so completely into oneself that only an abyss remains. In this context the famous "statue of nothing" in *Le Poète assassiné*, the void a half-meter wide and two meters deep which the dead poet's artist friend creates as a memorial (and Picasso, who realized that he was the friend, actually intended to make such a statue in Paris after Apollinaire's death), is more than a mere *sic transit gloria mundi* reflection; it becomes a terrifying glimpse into the void of the poet's own self. His rootlessness, the elusiveness of his identity must have made him sense that the thirst for total presence presupposes the state of total absence.

Miss Margaret Davies in her study on Apollinaire suggests that his "secret" was his feeling of inadequacy as a poet, his fear of poetic impotence; but if this were true how could the suffering become regenerative, as both "Tristesse d'une étoile" and "Les Collines" imply? Is the "secret" not rather the dread of the "abyss," the lucid awareness of which converts that dread into hope? Only by accepting the reality, the palpability of nothingness—and in a 1917 short story, "Mon cher Ludovic," Apollinaire speaks in fact of the solidity of the void—can the *nihil* become the fuel which feeds poetic ardor. One of the stanzas from "Les Collines" inscribed on his tomb in the Père Lachaise cemetery contains the following lines:

> Et j'ai scruté tout ce que nul
> Ne peut en rien imaginer
> Et j'ai soupesé maintes fois
> Même la vie impondérable
> Je peux mourir en souriant

Like the "statue en rien" of *Le Poète assassiné*, does not the "rien" of this passage suggest a solid substance?

Apollinaire never attempted to elaborate as a concept the dialectical thinking which lies beneath the simultanism and the polyvalence of his poetry. Nothing indicates that he had read Hegel; he knew Pascal and Nietzsche, but how extensively we cannot be sure. We have seen the influence of Mallarmé's poetics and the theories of cubism which made him formulate in his prose writings such paradoxes as the "truth within the lie," "clarity within obscurity," "humanity within inhumanity." Above all, however, it was through the very intimate and painful exploration of his own ambiguous nature that he evolved intuitively his multidirectional style. "One must have chaos in one," writes Nietzsche, "to give birth to a dancing star," and Apollinaire's victory as a poet sprang from the maze of contradictions within him as a man. Poets have understood at least since Heraclitus that "of everything that is true, the converse also is true," and time and again they have sought to pronounce "Odi et amo" in one breath. Yet the fact that the word "ambivalence" was not coined until 1916 is sufficient indication that the general acceptance of this concept is predominantly a twentieth-century acquisition. It is in this sense and not simply because he sang of the Eiffel Tower that Apollinaire is profoundly modern.

He once claimed that he would be happy with only seven readers: an American Negro boxer, an empress of China, a German journalist, a Spanish painter, a young woman of good French blood, an Italian peasant girl, and an English officer in India. In all modesty he thus seems to offer a prism that is only heptagonal, but as the reader on the lookout for a single facet comes across more and more, he suddenly discovers that the immediacy of these poems lies in the simultaneity of all the facets. And their universality as well, for Apollinaire assures us that we are as complex as he when in "Les Collines" he promises us secrets

> Qui se dévoileront bientôt
> Et feront de vous cent morceaux
> A la pensée toujours unique.

SELECTED BIBLIOGRAPHY

NOTE: *Apollinaire's poetry and theater appear in a complete one-volume edition, the* Oeuvres poétiques, *ed. Marcel Adéma and Michel Décaudin (Paris, Gallimard, Ed. de la Pléiade, 1956). A deluxe edition of the* Oeuvres complètes *in four volumes was published by Balland and Lecat, Paris, 1965–66. Selections in English may be found in* Selected Writings, *tr. Roger Shattuck (New York, New Directions, 1950) and* Selected Poems, *tr. Oliver Bernard (London, Penguin, 1965). Translations of individual volumes are listed below. For a detailed bibliography readers are referred to the Pléiade edition, supplemented by the annual issues since 1962 of* Guillaume Apollinaire *in* La Revue des Lettres Modernes (Paris, Minard).

PRINCIPAL WORKS OF GUILLAUME APOLLINAIRE

L'Enchanteur pourrissant. Paris, Kahnweiler, 1909.

L'Hérésiarque et Cie. Paris, Stock, 1910. (The Heresiarch and Company. Tr. Remy Inglis Hall. New York, Doubleday, 1965.)

Le Bestiaire ou Cortège d'Orphée. Paris, Deplanche, 1911.

Méditations esthétiques. Les Peintres cubistes. Paris, Figuière, 1913. (The Cubist Painters. Tr. Lionel Abel. New York, Wittenborn, Schultz, 1949.)

Alcools. Paris, Mercure de France, 1913. Paperback ed., Paris, Gallimard, Collection "Poésie," 1966. (Alcools. Tr. William Meredith; intro. and notes, Francis Steegmuller. New York, Doubleday, 1964. Alcools. Tr. Anne Greet. Berkeley–Los Angeles, University of California Press, 1965.)

Le Poète assassiné. Paris, L'Edition, Bibliothèque des Curieux, 1916. (The Assassinated Poet. Tr. Matthew Josephson. New York, Broom, 1923.)

Vitam impendere amori. Paris, Mercure de France, 1917.

Les Mamelles de Tirésias. Paris, Sic, 1918. (The Breasts of Tiresias. Tr. Louis Simpson. Odyssey, December, 1961.)

Calligrammes. Paris, Mercure de France, 1918. Paperback ed., Paris, Gallimard, Collection "Poésie," 1966.

La Femme assise. Paris, Nouvelle Revue Française, 1920.

Il y a. Paris, Messein, 1925.

L'Esprit nouveau et les poètes. Paris, Haumont, 1946. (The New Spirit and the Poets. Tr. Francis Steegmuller in Apollinaire: Poet Among the Painters. See below.)

Tendre comme le souvenir. Paris, Gallimard, 1952.

Le Guetteur mélancolique. Paris, Gallimard, 1952.
Poèmes à Lou. Geneva, Cailler, 1955. Revised edition of Ombre de mon amour, 1947.
Chroniques d'art (1902–1918). Ed. L. C. Breunig. Paris, Gallimard, 1961.

CRITICAL WORKS AND COMMENTARY

Adéma, Marcel. Guillaume Apollinaire. Paris, La Table Ronde, 1968.
Bates, Scott. Guillaume Apollinaire. New York, Twayne, 1967.
Bowra, C. M. The Creative Experiment. London, Macmillan, 1949.
Breunig, L. C. "Apollinaire's 'Les Fiançailles,'" Essays in French Literature, No. 3 (November, 1966).
Breunig, L. C., and J. C. Chevalier, Présentation de Guillaume Apollinaire. Les Peintres cubistes. Paris, Hermann, 1965.
Butor, Michel. "Monument de rien pour Apollinaire," Nouvelle Revue Française, Nos. 147, 148 (March-April, 1965).
Chevalier, J. C. "Apollinaire et le calembour," Europe, Vol. XLIV, No. 451–452 (November-December, 1966).
Davies, Margaret. Apollinaire. London, Oliver and Boyd, 1964.
Décaudin, Michel. La Crise des valeurs symbolistes. Toulouse, Privat, 1960.
—— Le Dossier d'Alcools. Paris, Minard, 1960.
Durry, Marie-Jeanne. Guillaume Apollinaire, Alcools. 3 vols. Paris, S.E.D.E.S., 1956–65.
Golding, John. "Guillaume Apollinaire and the Art of the Twentieth Century," The Baltimore Museum of Art News, Vol. XXVI, 4–Vol. XXVII, 1 (Summer-Autumn, 1963).
Lawler, James. "Apollinaire et La Chanson du Mal-Aimé," Australian Journal of French Studies, Vol. 1, No. 3 (September-October, 1964).
Lockerbie, S. I. "Alcools et le symbolisme," Guillaume Apollinaire 2 (Revue des Lettres Modernes, Nos. 85–89, Autumn, 1963).
Moulin, Jeanine. Guillaume Apollinaire, Textes inédits. Geneva, Droz, 1952.
Pia, Pascal. Apollinaire par lui-même. Paris, Seuil, 1954.
Raymond, Marcel. De Baudelaire au surréalisme. Paris, Corrêa, 1933.
Shattuck, Roger. The Banquet Years. New York, Harcourt, Brace, 1955.
Steegmuller, Francis. Apollinaire: Poet Among the Painters. New York, Farrar, Straus, 1963.

[48]